Voyagers

Upon the sea of life we sail
In ships we build of dreams,
We blindly steer a reckless course,
When charted by our schemes.

We sometimes sail for ports unknown,
When longing to be free,
And like the ancient mariner,
We sail the restless sea.

No port within the storm we find,
No refuge from the gale,
No friendly harbor looms in sight,
As on and on we sail.

But when the Master of the sea
Of life, our ships command,
His loving Hand will lead the way,
To guide us to safe land.

Julie E. Jones

Salesian Missions wishes to extend special thanks and gratitude to our generous poet friends and to the publishers who have given us permission to reprint material included in this book. Every effort has been made to give proper acknowledgments. Any omissions or errors are deeply regretted, and the publisher, upon notification, will be pleased to make the necessary corrections in subsequent editions.

First Edition Printed in the U.S.A. by Concord Litho Group., Inc., Concord, New Hampshire 03301-0464

The Voyage of Life

from the Salesian Collection

Compiled and edited by
Jennifer Grimaldi

Illustrated by
Russell Bushée, Frank Massa,
Maureen McCarthy, Paul Scully
and Robert VanSteinburg

Contents

I long to see God's springtime tree,
Green and adorned with blossoms free,
The dark of Winter finally past,
Warmth and light returned at last.
Hardy flowers bursting firm earth,
Fragrance and color announcing new birth,
Tulips awaken, emerging brand-new
To lift silken faces for kisses of dew.
Surely our Father meant springtime's fresh start
As a loving gift to gladden each heart.

Gael Phaneuf

Thank You, God

Thank You, God, for lovely Spring,
For miracles the season brings,
Each daffodil of brightest gold
And sunlight that my heart can hold,
For leaves to bless the naked trees
And every gentle Maytime breeze.

Thank You, God, for singing birds
That really need no human words,
For Nature's symphony of praise
And even April's rainy days,
For home and love and gentle care,
The smiling dawn – each evening prayer.

For longer days and less of dark,
The children playing in the park,
Each moment filled with hope and bliss,
The magic in a sunbeam's kiss,
For skies of blue and upturned sod,
From humble heart, I thank You, God.

Garnett Ann Schultz

April's a Child

April's a child who likes to play,
Catching bright sunbeams on her way,
Skipping across the vales and hills,
Waking the sleeping daffodils.

April's a child who likes to tease –
Sprinkling her showers, then to please,
Sending blue skies and golden sun,
Opening blossoms one by one.

April's a child in emerald gown,
Wearing a rainbow-ribboned crown,
Blessing us with her gentle charms,
Bringing us lilacs in her arms.

April's a child of song and mirth,
Spreading her joy o'er all the earth,
Thrilling our hearts to dance and sing,
Giving to us the gift of Spring.

Beverly J. Anderson

Come and see the works of God,
awesome in the deeds done for us.
Psalm 66:5

The Beauty of Spring

Lord, I am so wealthy,
I'm as rich as a king
Each time I awaken
To the beauty of Spring...

See a snow-covered mountain
Or a hill far away –
View a quaint, little chapel
Up the road just a way.

No wealth could quite measure
Or could ever compare
To the honor I'm feeling
When I kneel down in prayer.

Lord, I feel "oh so wealthy"
And I know I've been blessed
With the beauty and splendor
Of the world at its best.

Katherine Smith Matheney

Sweep the snow
And clean the ice,
Spring is coming to town.
To Winter, Winter,
We say, "goodbye"...
Too long it's been around.

She'll dress the trees
With buds and leaves
And flower all the land.
She'll bring with her
The peepers, bees...
She'll lead them by the hand.

Ready your heart
With gladsome song,
God's springtime soon we'll greet.
Welcome her here,
Make her belong...
Before she takes her leave.

Loise Pinkerton Fritz

...And Thou renewest
the face of the earth.
Psalm 104:30

Ritual of Spring

They shone like little amethysts
In fields behind our place,
Springtime's purple violets,
Each one, a nodding face...

And I in eager childhood days
Would run to pick bouquets
To put in Mother's outstretched hand
In happy days of May...

Sometimes I'd gather dandelions
With yellow fuzzy heads,
Mother seemed to love them so,
As much as blooms in beds...

And if I searched in earnest more,
A shooting star or two
Would be in my Spring offering,
Those special finds so few...

And all those lovely Maytime gifts
That to Mother I would bring,
Became a part and pleasure dear
In our ritual of Spring.

Virginia Borman Grimmer

The flowers appear on the earth,
the time of pruning the vines
has come, and the song of the
dove is heard in our land.
Solomon 2:12

Voyage

The sea of life is storm-tossed,
It's hard to stay afloat,
Whether we sail in mighty ships
Or row along in small boats.

Though we must sail through dark storms,
Billows may roll and thunder roar,
There is one Captain Who will guide
Us safely to the other shore.

Dovie A. Owens

The Lighthouse

There is a lighthouse near the shore
To guide the boats away
From sandbars and from rocks obscure
And lead them to the bay...
It has a strong and steady beam
That hovers o'er the tide;
However stormy it may seem,
The kindly light will guide...
It is the Father's caring,
Brightly gleaming on the waves,
That helps us keep our bearing,
It is His love that saves.
Look for the sturdy tower
That shines an unfailing ray
And points with heavenly power
To everlasting day.

Dorothy Didham

God in Nature

The beautiful fields of nature lie
Stretched out from here to yonder.
God put them here for you and me
To gaze upon and wonder.

We see the flowers come forth in Spring
From King Winter's desolation.
It makes us know that God is God
In all the many nations.

At night we see the beautiful stars
Light up the evening sky,
But that's just the outside of Heaven;
How beautiful it must be inside.

All around we can see God in nature.
We know One much greater than we
Orders the times and the seasons;
There is no other way it could be.

Wesley Yonts

Once Again It's Summertime

Once again it's summertime,
The skies above are blue.
The Summer bears such beauty
That calls to me and you.
The birds, they all are singing
A lovely roundelay,
The children shout with laughter
As they all run and play.
The flowers all are blooming
Way up there on the hill,
The waterwheel is turning
Down by the old gristmill.
I lift my hands to Heaven
To give Him thanks and praise,
The sun above is shining
With its warm, golden rays.
The chapel bells are pealing
Off in the nearby town,
And thus, the beauty of God
Is showing all around.

Mary E. Herrington

My Shepherd

I will not wander off, my Lord,
There is no dearer land
Than this wherein You labor
So watchful, staff in hand.

I will not leave You, Master,
But press closer in Your care,
There is no need of other worlds
Than Yours, so blessed, so fair.

You are the region of true peace,
There is no need to roam,
Your gentle grace surrounds me
And love becomes my home.

Bea Lotz

Then we, Your people, the sheep of Your pasture, will give thanks to You forever; through all ages we will declare Your praise.
Psalm 79:13

Home to Me

Home is more than a fresh coat of paint,
Crystal chandeliers or a garden of roses fair;
Plush carpets feel soft beneath the feet –
But, oh, the joy where love is shared!

To experience a hug and handshake
Weighs more than antiques and gold,
Leap into the precious moments of laughter
And become part of the "family" fold.

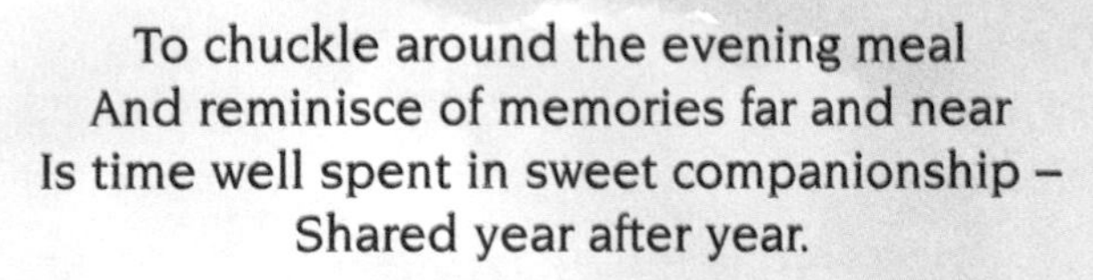

To chuckle around the evening meal
And reminisce of memories far and near
Is time well spent in sweet companionship –
Shared year after year.

Relish in the pride of a perfectly mowed lawn,
Polish the silver so fine,
But home to me is caring
By folks whose good virtues shine!

Linda C. Grazulis

Teach me to do Your will, for You are my God. May Your kind spirit guide me on ground that is level.
Psalm 143:10

Of Gracious Days

September dares to pose itself
In Summer's path to all
The leaves that turn in golden mists,
As Autumn comes to call.

October, shot with streaking flames
Of red and gold and brown,
And lemon, too, in graceful flight –
The leaves come wafting down.

November, fringed with nipping cool,
For Fall is everywhere;
A quietude of gracious days –
Thanksgiving's in the air.

Then all of a sudden Winter blows,
The snows are piling high;
I think of Autumn's calming hush –
A season passes by.

Henry W. Gurley

Amber Days of Autumn

In Autumn's breeze leaves tumble down,
Vermillion, crimson, bronze and brown.
The shim'ring oaks along the lane
Wear rainbow halos once again.

Bright bittersweet and woodbine twine,
Ripe grapes hang purpling on the vine.
Broad orchard trees stand bare and clean,
Their outstretched boughs no longer green.

Against the arching blue-hazed sky
The smoke-curled wreaths of bonfires fly.
Brown nuts drop to the leaf-strewn ground,
Where orange pumpkins now abound.

Full harvest moon-gold glazes all,
Night echoes crickets' farewell call.
We sing to God our hymn of praise
For His glorious gift of bright Autumn days.

Elisabeth Weaver Winstead

The earth has yielded its harvest;
God, our God, blesses us.
Psalm 67:7

A Change Is Coming

A change is coming, I can tell.
There's frost upon the wishing well.
The air is crisp as apple cider,
And leaves collect around the spider.

Her web holds fast throughout the night,
Spun silver bathed in pale moonlight.
The night's so clear, I just saw Mars
And wished upon a thousand stars!

No songbirds sing upon the hill;
They, too, have felt the north wind's chill.
No loons remain on golden pond
As Autumn waves her magic wand.

The rose and aster now are gone,
A coat of brown adorns each lawn.
A change is coming, and don't you know,
The hills will soon be white with snow.

Clay Harrison

You made the moon to mark the seasons,
the sun knows the hour of its setting.
Psalm 104:19

All Seasons His

Do you think that God made Autumn?
I know I hear His sound,
His whispered words, His shuffling walk
Upon His Summer's ground.

Do you think that God made Autumn?
I know I see His glow
In burnished suns, in harvest moons,
His first of season's snow.

Do you think that God made Autumn?
I know I feel the chills
Of drying winds, of early frosts
Upon His nearby hills.

Do you think that God made Autumn?
No surer fact there is!
And Winter – Spring – and Summer, too,
Are these – all seasons His!

Henry W. Gurley

With your own eyes you have seen all these great deeds the Lord has done.
Deuteronomy 11:7

Respite

The leaves are scudding through the air
And skipping down the busy street;
The Autumn air is crisp and cool
After Summer's trying heat.
My thoughts seem so beautiful,
Not going back nor rushing on,
And it's so peaceful here and now,
All my anxieties are gone.
No, it's not a fantasy,
Nor a very colorful daydream;
It's just a respite God can give!
Things are not what they seem,
But for this moment in the hearts
That turn to Him in loving prayer,
He grants this peace so we can work
For a like peace everywhere.

Dorothy Niederberger

The Beckoning

Once... it was fair, fair Summer,
Then Autumn... then it was gone,
We all had reminiscences
And dreams to dwell upon.

Winter whipped the landscape,
The wind turned flesh to blue,
And white had covered all the land
And trailed its fingers through.

Winter darkened skies of eve,
Lifted pleasantly the heart,
The coziness about the hearth
The gladness 'twould impart.
'Tis when life is beckoning
Old, quaint times of yore,
And, O', how haunting is the night
And years we've lived before.
James Joseph Huesgen

How Quiet and Deep the Stillness

How quiet and deep the stillness
Along by the forest trail,
When the soft whiteness of Winter
Lies spread over hill and dale.
Where ice-edged brooklets softly weep
Beneath the towering pines
That shatter the dreaming sunlight
Into shaft-like golden lines.
Where nothing is heard but the swishing boughs,
Or a lone crow faintly calling,
Or the flustered whir of a frightened deer,
Or a dead branch sharply falling.
Where the distant snow-draped mountains
Swim in the blue of the sky,
Where the wild winds coldly murmur
A wilderness lullaby.

Bernard D. Carroll

A Patch of Simple Faith

There's a patch of brightest emerald
Upon earth's darkened floor
As wintertime comes creeping in
And Autumn shuts its door.
It is a patch of greenest moss
That's hidden quite from sight,
But in the dark of wintertime
It's springtime's ray of light.

There is a patch of brightest hope
Within the Christian heart
When burdens press and cares distress
And earthly friends seem far.
It is a patch of simple faith
In Jesus Christ, our Lord;
Oh, when the moments darkest seem,
'Tis then His light shines forth.

Loise Pinkerton Fritz

An Awe-Inspiring Sight

When people speak of colors,
They seldom mention white,
But when Winter works her magic,
It's an awe-inspiring sight.

When the snow is gently falling
And all the landscape's white,
Earth's a portrait made in Heaven
When all is calm and bright.

It's a time for making snowmen
And angels in the snow
As the temperature keeps falling
And rivers cease their flow.

Icicles shine like crystals
In the purple twilight's glow,
And every cobweb is frosted
With flakes of ice and snow.

It's a time for celebration
When earth is colored white,
For when Winter works her magic,
It's an awe-inspiring sight!

Clay Harrison

It Must Be Spring

The birds that chirp and frolic
Tell me it must be Spring;
Their cheerfulness is catching
As my heart starts to sing.
I've longed the long, gray Winter
To greet sweet Spring anew,
To bid a hearty welcome
To azure skies of blue.
And so each morn I waken
To find a new surprise,
As precious gifts of nature
Appear before my eyes.

Catherine Janssen Irwin

A Whisper Came to Me

I feel so lost this very day –
Have I forgotten how to pray?
At dawn I woke sad and blue;
I didn't see green buds so new.

I didn't hear the robin's notes
Or observe how golden motes
Rode so delicately the breeze –
My heart was shut to all of these.

But soon a whisper came to me,
"Oh, My child, can't you see
How serene the sky above,
How My day smiles with love?"

I paused and opened wide my eyes
And saw how blue the Father's skies.
Then I prayed from bended knee
To earn the love He's given me.

Rosa Nelle Anderson

Spring's Unfolding Days...

Of all the seasons of the year
That call the heart to praise,
There's none I cherish more
Than Spring's unfolding days.

A dogwood tree on a hillside near
Bursts forth with blossoms gay;
Bright daffodils are nodding
Where lacy snowflakes lay.

The lawn is sprouting fresh and green,
Bathed with a dewy shine;
Small green leaves are peeping out
From bush and tree and vine.

The robin's morning hymn of praise
Neath sky of sapphire blue,
The smell of lilacs on rainwashed air
Brings Heaven close to you.

I think about His wonders,
How He sends the Spring anew;
And in my winter-weary heart,
I find renewal, too.

Kay Hoffman

Yet, in bestowing His *goodness,* He *did not leave*
Himself *without witness, for* He *gave you rains*
from Heaven *and fruitful seasons, and filled you*
with nourishment and gladness for your hearts.
Acts 14:17

Welcome, Spring!

God washed the world last night,
And made it fresh and clean again.
The rain gushed forth torrential tunes,
And brought the Winter to an end.

Hear the sound of singing streams,
Wisteria is clinging to the vine,
It hangs in veils of pearly blooms
To usher in a new springtime.

See the hawthorn white with Spring,
The robin as it hops along;
Each tree is filled with leaves of green,
And eggshells with potential song!

Hear the soft breeze as it whispers
Of the perfumed beauty it shall bring.
See neighbors peeping out their doors
To sweetly smile and welcome Spring!

Barbara Cagle Ray

Send Me a Beautiful Day

Take some golden sunshine,
Add a tranquil day in May,
Mix in roses and meadowlarks
And an ocean's salty spray.

Sprinkle tiny raindrops
From a misty morning sky,
Add scores of smiles and laughter,
Our lives to beautify.

Stir in the murmur of a brook
That sings Spring's melody;
Wrap them in the evening hush –
And send them all to me.

Nora M. Bozeman

He has made everything appropriate to its time, and has put the timeless into their hearts, without men's ever discovering, from beginning to end, the work which God has done.
Ecclesiastes 3:11

Here Comes April

I see April coming
And what an awesome sight
To see the branch all laden
With pink and peach and white.

The orchard is a dreamland
My eyes cannot believe;
How tell when I observe it
The message I receive?

For through the landscape Nature speaks
To tell me of God's love;
The blossom is the carrier
Of the dispatch from above.

It is a note of tender care
In which it's understood
When God and I are in commune
Must all things work for good.

Thus April is a special month
That makes the heart sincere
To read the hopeful greeting
He mails this time of year.

Don Beckman

...great and wonderful are all Your
works, Lord God almighty.
Revelations 15:3

A Child Should Live

A child should live where violets grow
To greet the early Spring,
Where there are fields that they can roam
And hear the birds that sing,
To find a hilltop reaching high,
A magic country lane,
Enjoying all the miracles
While walking in the rain.
A child should live where Nature dwells
Beneath the Summer sun,
To chase the wind in happiness
And wade in creeks that run,
To feel the grass beneath their feet
That tickles tiny toes,
Where they can romp in joyful peace
While sunbeams kiss their nose.
Perhaps to learn of growing things,
To know of Nature's charms,
To find the miracles of life,
A kitten in their arms,
The very special hidden place
Where laughter fills each heart,
A child should live in peace and love
That moments sweet impart.

Garnett Ann Schultz

A Mother's Prayer

Lord, please bless my children,
Protect them day and night;
Lead them down the right roads,
Forever in Thy sight.

Let them know Thy presence
Each step along the way,
Giving strength and courage
To sustain them, come what may.

Be their consolation
In times of woe and strife,
Guide them past the pitfalls
On their journey thru this life.

And when this life is over,
See them safely to that shore,
Where peace and love are boundless
Beyond Heaven's golden door.

Catherine Janssen Irwin

The Child grew and became strong,
filled with wisdom; and the favor
of God was upon Him.
Luke 2:40

A Beacon of Love

God's love is like a beacon
That can cause an inner glow,
It can reach in hidden corners,
Making them just overflow.

His love can dispel sorrow,
Help a broken heart to heal,
Giving us a great assurance
That the love of God is real.

We can also be a beacon
As we go from day to day,
Casting love beams around us,
Pointing others to the way.

Lifting someone who has fallen,
Showing faith instead of doubt,
Telling people if they need us,
We'll be glad to help them out.

As the love of God surrounds us,
Bringing grace to aid in strife,
May our love shine like a beacon,
And continue all through life.

Frances Culpe Wolfe

Guide me in Your truth and teach me, for You are God my Savior, and for You I wait all the day.
Psalm 25:5

Time to Grow

Every tree we want to prosper
Must have time to grow;
Every form must learn to weather
Trials of wind and snow;
Give it time to gain – through hardships –
Strength to fight distress,
Let the warmth of many Summers
Bathe it in caress.

Do not rush the growing season,
For a tree to bear;
Let it, slowly, grow and ripen;
Nourish it with care.
Fruits of limb – like mind and body –
Ripen to their best,
If they are allowed to ripen
Without being pressed.

Michael Dubina

He Will Light Your Way

When you have no place to turn
And you are in despair,
Just look into your heart and soul,
For God is always there.

Remember that He loves you
And will listen to your prayer,
And He will give you comfort
And ease each trial you bear.

As long as you have faith and hope
He'll always stay with you,
Dispelling all the gloom you feel
Until the day is through.

And when you wake up in the morn
To start a brand-new day,
Remember God is with you,
And He will light your way.

Dolores Karides

Light is sweet! And it is pleasant
for the eyes to see the sun.
Ecclesiastes 11:7

God, Take Control

God, take control from this day forth
Of me and all I own,
My triumphs and my failures,
Which belong to Thee alone.
Rid me of all delusions,
That I am brave and strong,
Show me how much I need You
To help me get along.
God, take control of everything
That has to do with me,
Restore the sight within my soul,
That I may truly see.
Mend what I have broken
And cannot now repair,
And when my heart feels empty,
Remind me You are there.
God, take control, things don't work out,
The times I get my way,
You always know what's best for me
Through every night and day.
And just because of all the love
Within my heart for Thee,
I humbly pray you'll always be
... Responsible for me!

Grace E. Easley

Simple Acts of Kindness

Simple acts of kindness
Can help the sun to shine,
They deserve our appreciation
So on them daily let us dine!

Offering someone a ride
On a rainy day,
Or a smile can uplift
When there's not a word to say.

A cup of coffee and a visit,
Cookies shared when freshly baked,
A handshake or a friendly hug
Can refresh the heart that aches.

Simple acts of kindness
That God created patiently from above,
And we are but His tiny vessels
Filled to share these acts of love!

Linda C. Grazulis

Shadows

The lingering shadows of Summer
Are giving way to those of Fall.
They seem to hover around the yard
And climb the garden wall.

They appear as if by magic,
They're much like abstract art.
The lines are bent and broken,
At times they split apart.

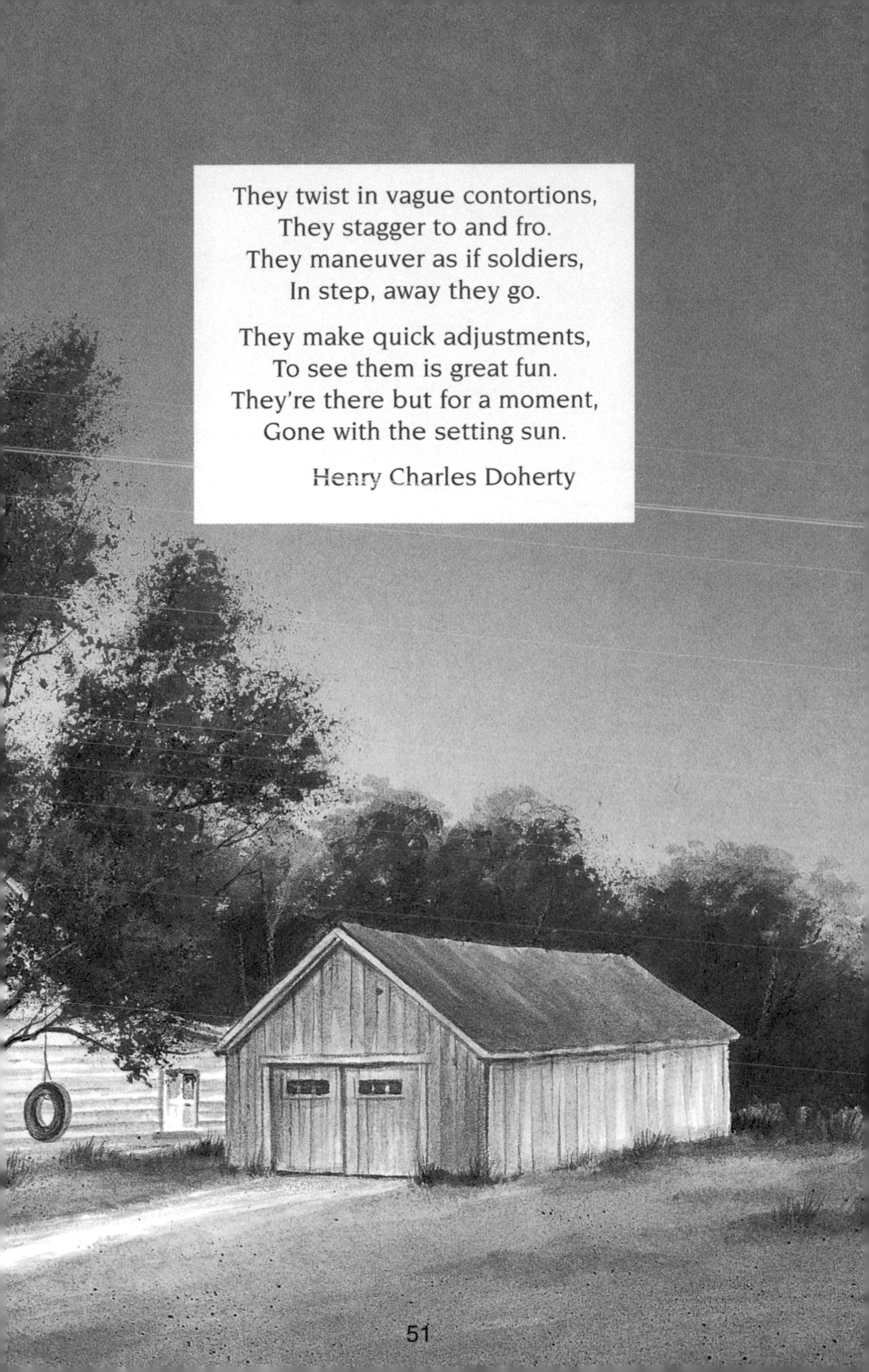

They twist in vague contortions,
They stagger to and fro.
They maneuver as if soldiers,
In step, away they go.

They make quick adjustments,
To see them is great fun.
They're there but for a moment,
Gone with the setting sun.

Henry Charles Doherty

Colorful Ballet

The Autumn leaves come tumbling down
In yellow, orange, red and brown.
They skip and waltz and gently glide
As on the crispy breeze they ride.

We watch with joy this Autumn day
Their twirling, colorful ballet.
Their merry trip to earth complete,
They make a carpet for our feet.

Beverly J. Anderson

The Lord look upon you
kindly and give you peace!
Numbers 6:26

The Sermon of the Trees

The trees proclaim God's majesty
When Autumn walks the land.
They fill my eyes with beauty
Too grand to understand.

Each poplar's a cathedral
With spires of shiny gold;
Each maple wears a crimson robe
That's lovely to behold.

Each path is a patchwork quilt
When leaves begin to fall.
My heart is overflowing
With the wonder of it all.

I pause to make a memory
Of moments such as these,
Knowing I have been blessed
By the sermon of the trees.

Clay Harrison

Autumn

The air is brisk, the days grow short,
The morning air is cold.
The leaves on the trees are colored bright
With hues of red, yellow and gold.
The harvest moon shines at night,
Sunsets are gold and red.
A touch of frost is in the air,
Stars shine bright overhead.
Fall is the time when God gets ready
To put all Nature to sleep.
And now's the time to enjoy
The fruits of harvest we've reaped.
God's Nature is colored in brightest hues;
To take a walk is a pleasure.
Enjoy it now before it fades,
And make a memory to treasure.

Grace Lewis

Changing of the Guard

There's a changing of the guard,
For Summer's on the wane,
And Autumn's slowly strolling
Down a country lane.

For tips of leaves show scarlet,
Sometimes fronds of gold,
As days grow so much shorter,
The weather becomes bold.

I batten down the hatches,
Store the larder to the hilt,
Savor sunny mornings
When the sun drops flakes of gilt.

I put away my Summer thoughts
And preen my mind for Fall,
As I gather downy milkweed pods
And hear the wild geese call.

Virginia Borman Grimmer

Fill us at daybreak with Your love,
that all our days we may sing for joy.
Psalm 90:14

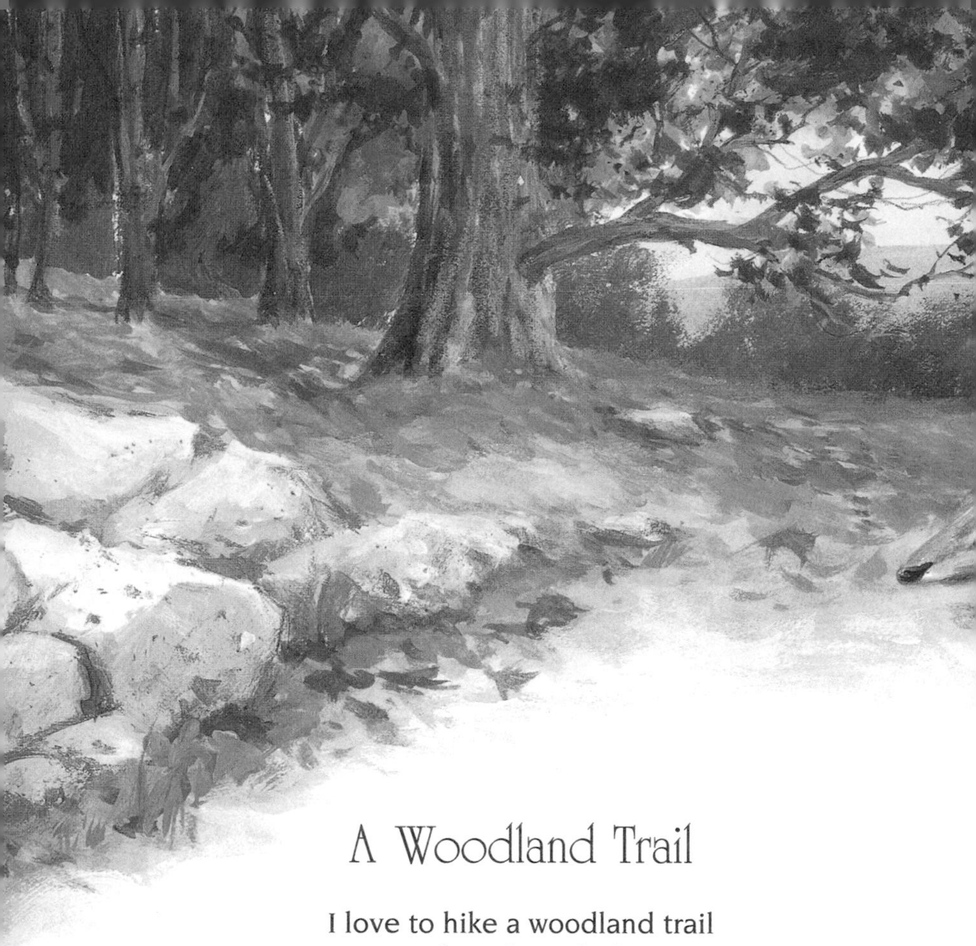

A Woodland Trail

I love to hike a woodland trail
As it wanders through the trees,
It brings me true contentment
And puts my very soul at ease.

The forest is so peaceful
And I love its cooling shade,
And I feel so meek and humble
In this arbor God has made.

I can feel a certain magic
In that cool, refreshing air,
As I seek the many secrets
That the forest wants to share.

I love to move real slowly
As I quietly make my way,
And watch to see what wonders
God unfolds for me this day.

I love to hike a woodland trail,
It brings a welcome peace to me,
And I thank our great Creator
For this soothing serenity.

Louis J. Kacinko

...He guides me in right paths
for His name's sake.
Psalms 23:3

God's Creatures Small

A snow has fallen overnight
And looks so beautiful and right;
There are footprints running to and fro
As if they knew not where to go.

It must have surely been a hare –
God's creatures beautiful and rare;
I used to track them in the snow
When as a child of long ago.

I'd wonder where they had been,
These small and furry rabbit friends;
I knew God cared for them so much,
He gave them shelter for a hutch.

God cares for everything the same,
Oh, bless His precious, holy name;
And like His creatures in the snow,
He's cared for us since long ago.

Katherine Smith Matheney

Before the Drift

Soft, white, fleecy snowdrops
Pouring from the sky,
Madly hurrying and bustling,
The flaky jewels fly.

Gently dropping everywhere
On bush and leaf and tree,
Fugitives from God's firmament
That fall relentlessly.

The tree of clouds called Heaven
Stretching up above us all
Sends down these snowbud blossoms,
On earth like jewels they fall.

Erna Gwillim

The Snow Outside My Window

White canvas of beauty
Sent from above,
Softly, tenderly
Expressing God's love...

A love so pure,
A grace so free,
All Nature looks up
With praise to Thee.

His spirit has touched
The white canvas below,
Painting a picture
That others may know.

The Master's touch,
Forgiveness from sin,
A heart that's aglow
With a reverence for Him.

Seek His presence,
Experience His power,
Meet the Master
This very hour.

White canvas of beauty
Sent from above,
Softly, tenderly,
Expressing God's love.

Connie Bosher

God's Winter Wonders

Outside the window crystal bright,
The silent world wears winter-white,
Frost flowers frame the panes of glass
To mirror chickadees that pass.

High above the gray fencerow,
In the splintered sunlight's glow,
Icicles hang from woodland trees
And pirouette in wintry breeze.

White lamb-clouds skim the dappled sky,
As silver snowbirds flutter by,
Beneath the cedar's frozen lace,
An ermine rug is tucked in place.

The snowflake stars spin softly down
In dazzling beauty to the ground,
A portrait of Nature's white wonderland
Is gloriously painted by God's great hand.

Elisabeth Weaver Winstead

His Praises Do I Sing

Our heavenly Father loveth all,
However bad or good;
But if we give our hearts to Him,
By Him we're understood.

For God, our Father, knoweth well
Of every joy and pain;
And through His tender love for us,
We're strengthened and sustained!

My Father, God, oh hear me now,
As I draw near to Thee;
For evermore to praise Thy name,
That all Thy wonders see!

Sancie Earman King

Anticipation

By my window sits a redbird,
In my heart there is a song;
Though the Winter winds are sweeping,
Spring will be here before long.
Let the sunshine keep on hiding
Behind dark clouds, drifting low;
I see blossoms in the treetops.
Flowers pushing through the snow,
Green grass covering the meadows,
Daffodils upon a hill...
Dreams of sunshine and of flowers
In the midst of Winter's chill.

Regina Wiencek

If You Should Call

If it happened You should call me, Lord,
Amid the noise and clamor of the day,
Intent upon my troubles and my plans,
Distracted by what lay along the way.
If You should whisper in my ear of all
I missed in life by being less like Thee,
And tell me with a little fortitude
I could become what I was meant to be.
If You should coax me gently with a smile
To follow in Your steps, to lean upon
Thy heart alone, forsaking lesser loves,
Mine today, perhaps tomorrow gone…
Oh, Lord, if You should whisper in my ear,
Do You suppose I'd have the sense to hear?

Grace E. Easley

The First Day of Spring

The Winter door closes,
Spring's door stands ajar,
And there in her beauty,
I see her each March.

She skips through the meadows
Where wild seeds lie in wait
To greet her, the princess
Of blossoming days.

She wanders through forests
With moss-covered floors,
She scales every mountain,
Strokes God's out-of-doors.

She tiptoes through gardens,
Brings birds on the wind,
I welcome her gladly...
The first day of Spring.

Loise Pinkerton Fritz

For, lo, the Winter is past, the rain is over and gone; the flowers appear on the earth; the time of the singing of birds is come, and the voice of the turtle is heard in our land.
Song of Solomon 2:11-12

Planting a Garden

When we're planting a garden,
There is something we should know,
It takes good seed and weeding
If our garden is to grow.

And so it is in life,
Deep within your heart and mine,
We are planting there a garden
To last through all of time.

Seeds of kindness and of love,
Tended daily with a prayer,
Will keep the garden in our heart
Forever blooming fair.

But should we become neglectful,
Of this is no doubt,
The weeds of selfishness and greed
Will crowd the good seeds out.

To be a happy gardener,
Plant only good seeds there,
Then weed and feed it faithfully
With tender loving care.

Kay Hoffman

Cast all your worries upon Him
because He *cares for you.*
1 Peter 5:7

The Joys of Spring

I so look forward to the Spring
When flowers bloom and birds take wing,
Dormant meadows come alive
And trout to mountain streams arrive.

I so look forward to the Spring
With all its cheerful happenings –
From Easter bonnets with their frills,
To ducks and chicks and daffodils.

I so look forward to the Spring,
I see God's love in everything,
Winter's nippy bite is past
And we can greet the sun at last.

Catherine Janssen Irwin

The Colors of Spring

The colors of Spring are cheerful and bright,
A most welcomed change from Winter's stark white.

From daffodil yellow, to robin's egg blue,
All nature's a rainbow of every hue.

The roses awaken from blankets of snow,
And the grass is green wherever we go.

From hollyhock pink, to butterfly gold,
The colors of Spring are a sight to behold!

Clay Harrison

This is the day the Lord has made;
let us rejoice and be glad.
Psalm 118:24

This Day Is Mine

This day is mine with its sunshine rare,
The sky so blue and the hills so fair,
The brook at play in the quiet dawn,
The whole wide world I can gaze upon.

This day is mine with its joys complete,
The springtime flowers with their fragrance sweet,
The spreading trees and the hope they bring,
Each little bird with a song to sing.

Oh, yes, God says that this day is mine,
To have and to keep 'til the end of time,
The mem'ries rich, such a treasured part,
So much in beauties to thrill my heart.

This day is mine with so much I love,
All Mother Nature I'm dreaming of,
From the solid earth to the heavens fair,
This day is mine with its joy and care.

Garnett Ann Schultz

Blessed day by day be the Lord,
Who bears our burdens; God,
Who is our salvation.
Psalm 68:20

God on Display

Through the amber of the sunset,
Through the lilacs on display,
Through the diamond in each dewdrop,
These are splendors of His ways.

Through the orchestra of magic,
Down the babbling, crystal stream,
In the rainbow's work of wonder,
In all these, God can be seen.

In the soft, warm breeze of evening,
In united hearts of friends,
These are gifts so freely given
And a joy for Him to send.

So just look around about you
For God is on display,
You will recognize Him clearly
By the splendor of His ways.

Chris Zambernard

Today I Walked on the Beach With a Friend

Thank You for the blessings of this day,
For letting me try in some small way
To ease the burden another bears
And help to shoulder another's cares.

The paths that are walked alone no more
Cannot seem so fearful as before
To the one who struggles with his grief
And offers thanks for blessed relief.

The breeze that blows on the sapphire shores
Cleanses the heart and the soul restores.
The wavelets cool have kissed our feet,
And You have shown life, again, is sweet.

Marjorie J. Lockhart

God's Brushstrokes

Your life is like a canvas
On which God paints for you
A waterfall of lessons
Filled with grace and truth.

His brushstrokes will be varied
With soft hues and some bold,
Which gradually create a scene
As your life unfolds.

Some patchwork may show sunshine,
A spattering – some rain.
He shades and washes with His brush
Your sorrows, joys and pain.

If perhaps your canvas seems
Confusing from the start,
Trust God to turn it into
A splendid work of art.

Your completed picture
Will be beautiful as planned,
If you'll be opened to the touch
Of the Master's loving hand.

Joyce Mary Ecochard

May He grant you what is in your heart and fulfill your every plan.
Psalm 20:5

Hands of Care

There is a touch of magic
In hands of loving care
That heal the wounds of heartache
And comfort – in despair;
They soothe the pains of suffering
And calm the fears of life,
And dry the tears of graying years
That dampen age of strife.
They are the gentle hands of grace
That God has willed us all –
To ease each other's aches and pains
And ease each other's falls.
When herbs and medicines of life,
No longer ease despair,
There is a touch of magic
In hands of loving care.

Michael Dubina

More and More

Lord, always be at home within my heart,
Let Your presence flood across my soul,
Let's play hide-and-seek like children do,
And let me find You quickly, for behold,
Apart from You I am alone and lost.
So used to Your dear presence I have grown,
Put Your hand upon my heart and feel
How strong the beats, and all for You alone.

How precious are these moments that we share
When we merge together and are one,
How intimate the words I hear You speak,
And I am awed at all that You have done.
Let me wake up loving You and then,
Let me fall asleep within Your heart,
Take my will and all that I possess,
And grant the two of us shall never part.

Through Your eyes my own have learned to see
How great the poverty that I possess,
My nothingness that merits not a thing,
Yet You bend down to love me, nonetheless.
There is a breathless flutter in my soul,
A sudden yearning never felt before,
For though I love You, Lord, with all my strength,
I always want to love You more and more!

Grace E. Easley

At the Sea

I'm going down to the sea,
Away from the busy world,
Down where the waves are calm,
And the flag of calm is unfurled.

With book in hand, I'll stroll along
And meditate the more,
The while I watch the sea gulls
And feel my soul restored.

I'll find a cool and restful place,
Sit there awhile and read,
Always from the Bible,
And gain just the food I need.

Jesus always loved the sea,
He preached upon its shore,
And fed the hungry multitudes
Food they had not known before.

Not just for the body,
He fed to make them whole
By giving them the sustenance
To satisfy their souls.

And so I'll think of Him today,
He's always on my mind,
That like unto those others,
Healing through His word I'll find.

Don Beckman

Life's Colors

Life has its many colors
And its ever-changing hues,
A kaleidoscope of images,
Of people, places, too.
A patchwork filled with memories,
Each stitched within our minds,
A way we can return
To other places, other times.
Life has its many colors,
Some light and bright and gay,
While others are much darker,
Like brown and black and gray.
Each color has its time and place,
Life's a mixture of them all,
Like the colors that we find
Of the leaves on trees in Fall.
Life has its many colors,
Each touch our lives and then,
The color wheel keeps turning,
And life changes once again.

Gina Mazzullo Laurin

September Flight

On this bright September morn,
I know it won't be very long
Before my little feathered friends
Will take to flight as Summer ends.

Their frolicking and plumage bright
Will sadly disappear from sight,
And I can't help but feel forlorn,
For I'll miss their cheerful song.

But, come the Spring, I'll find once more
The happiness they'll hold in store,
For ever-watchful, anxious me,
As they settle in my old oak tree.

Catherine Janssen Irwin

How manifold are Your works, O Lord!
In wisdom You have wrought them all –
the earth is full of Your creatures.
Psalm 104:24

Let Go – Let God

When life seems overbearing,
And it pains your heart and soul…
Let go… let God become your Master.
Put yourself in His control.

If trouble comes and you are weary,
Torn with guilt and with regret,
Let go… let God embrace your spirit.
He has already paid your debt.

When affliction mars your vision,
And you're wallowing in fear…
Let go… let God… He will protect you.
Know that He is always near.

If others hurt, malign your spirit,
You can walk in faith and pride,
Let go... let God, for He has promised
All your needs will be supplied.

When your world abounds in sorrow,
And depression leaves its mark,
Let go... let God bring light and laughter.
He alone can light the dark.

If you're bound in chains and shackles,
Warped and wrapped in worldly things...
Let go... let God release your bondage.
He will give your heart new wings.

Patience Allison Hartbauer

Portrait of Fall

Looking out my window
In October's golden light,
I see a beauty unsurpassed,
A truly lovely sight.

Leaves are saying soft good-byes,
As they come floating down,
To make a nature's carpet
Of yellow, red and brown.

Mountaintops, now turned to white,
Forewarn of Winter's chills,
While trees, like golden rivers,
Wind their way up through the hills.

Throughout our world's creation,
You will ever find it thus,
Kaleidoscopes of color,
In God's hand, the Artist's brush.

Alora M. Knight

Give thanks to the Lord, invoke His name; make known among the nations His deeds. Sing to Him, sing His praise, proclaim all His wondrous deeds.
1 Chronicles 16:8-9

Autumn's Own Colors

I love all the summertime
Scenes so exciting,
But Autumn's own colors
Are all so inviting.

The russet-brown hues
Of the autumntime fair,
And the chill of the morning's
Own autumntime air.

The scenes from the hillside,
All dressed out in splendor,
Seems Summer has chosen
The sweetest surrender.

And before very long,
As the seasons all go,
All the hills, dales and mountains
Will be covered with snow.

Katherine Smith Matheney

Leaves

I stood alone on a wooded hill,
Shivering in the nip of a late Autumn chill,
Sadly I watched in the cool, crisp air,
As nature's trees grew steadily bare.

I could hear the angry, rustling breeze
Whistling through the lonely trees,
Scattering leaves of red and gold,
That were dropped by the millionfold.

Through the air, they gaily whirled,
On the ground, they wildly swirled,
'Til at last they came to rest
In this, their final, wintry nest.

Soon these trees will fall asleep
'Mid piles of leaves so very deep,
And await the Winter snows to fall,
To softly blanket them one and all.

The snows will come and drifts will grow,
'Mid howling winds that gust and blow,
'Til Mother Nature does decide
'Tis time for Winter to subside.

When Winter snows are finally gone,
The buds of Spring will then be born,
New leaves will happily then appear,
Which nature provides each passing year.

These buds will soon grow big and strong
And cling to Mother all season long,
As she proudly spreads her arms that hold
Her countless children within her fold.

All season long, she will proudly display
Her beautiful offspring day after day,
'Til again the Autumn winds will blow,
To loudly remind us of forthcoming snow.

Joseph Ferrara

From Dawn to Dusk

From dawn throughout the evening,
The little birds I hear,
Their songs so very soothing,
Each note so sweet and clear.

Dear Father, up in Heaven,
If only I could sing
With purity and sweetness,
Just like the birds on wing.

Dear Father, Thee I worship
Throughout each bright day long,
My heart to be Thy dwelling,
For I to Thee belong!

Sancie Earman King

Shout joyfully to God, all you on earth,
sing praise to the glory of His *name;*
proclaim His *glorious praise.*
Psalm 66:2

Hope for Tomorrow

We all face these seasons
Of heartache and pain,
We find our dreams shattered
And prayers seem vain.
With hope disappearing,
The heart has no song,
We're waiting for daybreak,
But the night is so long.

There is hope for tomorrow,
God is still in control,
He will not forsake us,
But keeps watch o'er our souls.
God holds our tomorrow,
Why should we despair?
He counts every teardrop
And hears every prayer.

Regina Wiencek

Walking With God

I traveled down a lonely road,
The way was dark and bitter cold,
There was no one to share my load,
No loving hand for me to hold.

I stopped inside God's house one day,
Despair led me to call His name,
And as I knelt to humbly pray,
Into my heart the Savior came.

So now I walk the shores of time,
No longer lonely, but complete,
For One Whose love is so divine
Doth gently guide my weary feet.

Ruth Gillis

Snowflakes

Snowflakes come like magic,
They seem to dance and sing,
It seems just like a miracle
As they cover everything.

Each snowflake seems so special
As they come from Heaven above,
God covers each and every thing
To show us His great love.

It seems just like a wonderland
At each and every glance,
And diamonds seem to sparkle
With snow on every branch.

Yes, snowflakes come like magic
In a special kind of way,
It seems that God is saying,
"Have a very special day."

Bonnie J. Knapp

Mother Nature's Valentine

Winter waved her magic wand
One February night –
In the morning all the earth
Was robed in dazzling white.

Silently Jack Frost had come,
And with his special flair,
Crystal-trimmed each shrub and tree,
Etched windows everywhere.

Winter left her calling card
Of fairyland design –
Frosty white and ribbon-laced...
Her fancy valentine.

Beverly J. Anderson

As long as the earth lasts, seedtime and harvest, cold and heat, Summer and Winter, and day and night shall not cease.
Genesis 8:22

Cardinal Guest

There's no more welcomed Winter guest
Than redbird with his vivid crest.
Resplendent gem in crystal snow,
He lights, puffs plumage up just so,
To shield him from the frosty cold
And bring his viewers joy untold!

Observe him quietly, he won't mind,
He's seldom shy of humankind.
A scarlet bloom on frozen lace,
He lends to Winter, Summer's grace.
His blazing beauty fires the heart
With gratitude for living art.

Louise Pugh Corder

How precious is Your love, O God!
We take refuge in the shadow of Your wings.
Psalm 36:8

Transformations

Quickly masking all with beauty –
Huge flakes of snow drift down,
As if white clouds were breaking up
And cov'ring all the ground!
It swallows bushes, fences, the road –
Any nook it can discover:
Enveloping all, not showing favor,
With its lovely, marshmallow cover!

Even the trash is looking nice –
Waiting patiently there,
With its curlicues and fingers gloved,
Upheld in the frozen air.
The woodpile, too, the backyard denizen –
Before just tending to duty,
Is soon completely encased in white,
Joining the parade of beauty!
Such transformations reminding me of
The promise Jesus has given
Of sins of scarlet made white as snow,
The reason He came from Heaven!

Lynn Fenimore Nuzzi

Pick a Pretty, Bright Bouquet

Winter seems to be all spent,
April showers due,
Lovely flowers will take a stand
In a day or two.

Open wide their beauty rare,
Misting sweet perfume,
Pick a pretty, bright bouquet,
Decorate the room.

Lovely flowers in a vase
Touched with beauty rare,
Tender blossoms to behold
In God's loving care.

Some by human hand are sown,
Other flowers grand,
Planted in a barren field
By the Master's hand.

Katherine Smith Matheney

I Thank Thee

Dear Lord, I thank Thee on this day
For all Thy loving care;
I thank Thee for Thy holy name
And I kneel to Thee in prayer...

Dear Lord, I thank Thee on this day
For hope and faith and love;
I open up my heart and soul
And reach to Thee above...

Dear Lord, I thank Thee on this day
For giving me Thy hand;
And should I falter, precious Lord,
Help me to understand!

Hope C. Oberhelman

So Much God Gives

God shows His love at dawning,
In birdsong symphonies,
In warming rays of sunshine
That filter through the trees.
In soft and balmy breezes,
Grass sparkling with the dew,
In many ways God whispers,
"I made this world for you."

He gives us gifts of beauty,
Surrounding day by day,
The flowers in the gardens,
The wildflowers by the way.
The sky so blue above us
With fluffy clouds of white,
Gay butterflies that soar by
And thrill us with delight.

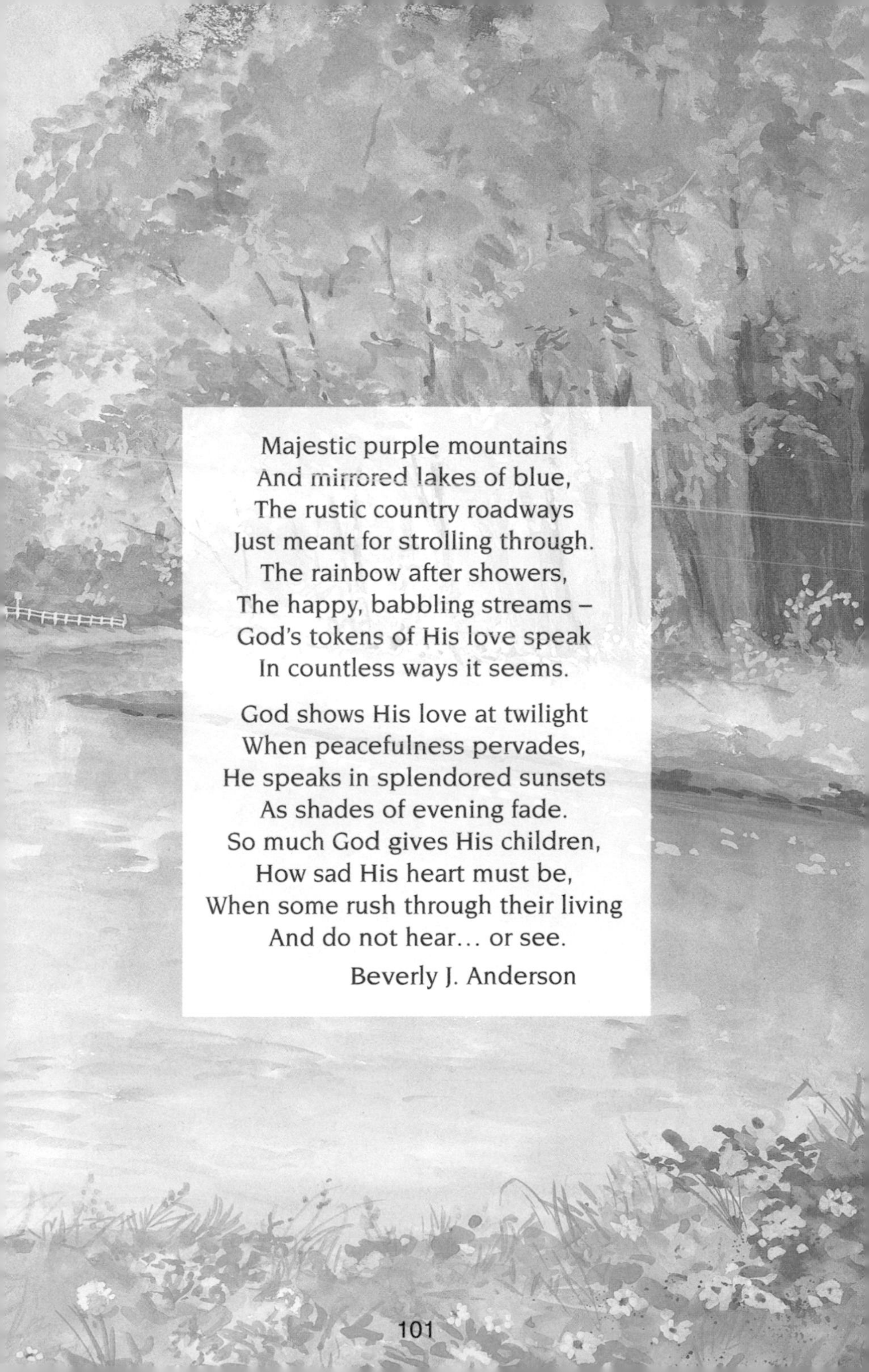

Majestic purple mountains
And mirrored lakes of blue,
The rustic country roadways
Just meant for strolling through.
The rainbow after showers,
The happy, babbling streams –
God's tokens of His love speak
In countless ways it seems.

God shows His love at twilight
When peacefulness pervades,
He speaks in splendored sunsets
As shades of evening fade.
So much God gives His children,
How sad His heart must be,
When some rush through their living
And do not hear... or see.

Beverly J. Anderson

Rememb'ring

Rememb'ring heals the deepest wounds
And soothes each aching heart,
While all the joys that one recalls
Are gifts that God imparts.

Rememb'ring cannot stay the lash,
But softens life's cruel blows,
And tho it can't remove the thorns,
It helps one see the rose.

Rememb'ring's gentle, loving touch
Is all one really needs
To find the lovely flowers that
Are hidden in the weeds.

So when you feel your burdens are
A bit too much to bear,
Just search your heart, rememb'ring that
The answer lies in there.

Sister Miriam Barker, C.D.S.

Spring Celebration

How blue is the sky above blossoming hillsides?
How green is the grass in the meadows below?
A fragrant breeze caresses the treetops,
Petals are falling, soft as the snow.

Throughout the valley, new life is emerging,
Flowers unfold in the warmth of the sun.
Birds have returned, the air's filled with singing,
Winter is gone and Spring has begun.

All Nature joins in the glad celebration,
Giving of thanks to our Maker above.
He showers the earth with wondrous beauty,
Great is His wisdom, unchanging His love.

Regina Wiencek

*Give thanks to the Lord,
for He is good, for His
kindness endures forever.*
Psalm 106:1

The Color Green

Green could be God's favorite color,
To cool the earth in shade,
In grass and trees and flowers,
On the earth that our God made.

The beautiful colors of butterflies,
Pretty birds and everything,
Relieve the monotony of drab colors,
In the blessing our God brings.

A spectacular sunset in the west,
No mere man can duplicate,
Only in the realm of the glory of God,
Can colors in His love relate.

The blue-green of the ocean, white-capped waves,
Drifting white clouds 'neath skies of blue,
In earth and sky, a melody
God gave to me and you.

When the storm clouds come rolling in
On the dark side of our life,
After each rain, the sun will shine,
In faith, we can overcome dark nights.

The rain over hills and valleys
Will life renew each time,
Tears like the rain will renew your life,
If God's love you seek to find.

Gene Koons

Blessed is the man who trusts in the Lord, whose hope is the Lord. He is like a tree planted beside the waters that stretches its roots to the stream: It fears not the heat when it comes, its leaves stay green...
Jeremiah 17:7-8

The Joyful Heart

When we are feeling saddened,
We need not stay that way,
For God, our Father, loves us
And hears us when we pray.

We seek our heavenly Father,
Tho earth's light may be dim,
For sweet it is to worship,
And thus commune with Him.

So let us never worry,
For we need never part
From God, our heavenly Father,
Who gives the joyful heart!

Sancie Earman King

I See You, Lord

I see You in the flowers,
I hear You in the trees,
I feel Your awesome presence
In the cool and gentle breeze.

I see You in the smile
Of a peaceful, joyful face,
I feel that You are with me,
As I bow my head for grace.

Help me, Lord, to rest in You
And treasure all my days,
For if I get too busy,
I'll miss Your choice bouquets.

Frances Gregory Pasch

You will show me the path of life, fullness of joys in Your presence, the delights at Your right hand forever.
Psalm 16:11

God Is With Us

God works in strange and wondrous ways
To show us what our powers can be,
How we can conquer pain and strife,
How we can plainly see

That He is with us day by day,
And through the darkest night,
That somewhere in the future,
We'll see the brightest light.

God is always with us
To lead us right along
That straight and narrow path,
To show us right from wrong.

If we will only heed Him,
Listen to His command,
Join hands with His armed forces
To that Glory Land.

If we give our hand to Jesus
And let Him lead us where
His blessed, holy Father
Is waiting for us there.

Lucille West

A Summer Prayer

On a hot, steamy day,
I put my lawn chair in the shade,
Lean back and relax,
With a glass of lemonade.

I look out on the well-kept lawn,
Close-cropped of emerald green,
I spy daylilies by the pond,
A stunning, picturesque scene.

I turn my face toward
The cloudless sky above,
The comforting muted shades of blue
Reassure me of His love.

I pray, "Dear Lord, guide me
In everything I do,
Help me to remember…
I am nothing without You!"

Nell Ford-Hann

Today I Saw a Hummingbird

Today I saw a hummingbird,
And how it blessed my life,
For one brief, shining moment,
I forgot my stress and strife.

It paused among the hollyhocks
'Til its wings began to hum,
And then it flew beyond the trees
Of cherry, peach and plum.

I thought how delicate this bird –
How fragile, too, is life,
Which comes and goes so quickly,
We're caught up in the strife.

Take time to smell the flowers, friend,
Enjoy each newborn day –
For life lingers like that hummingbird,
Then flies silently away.

Clay Harrison

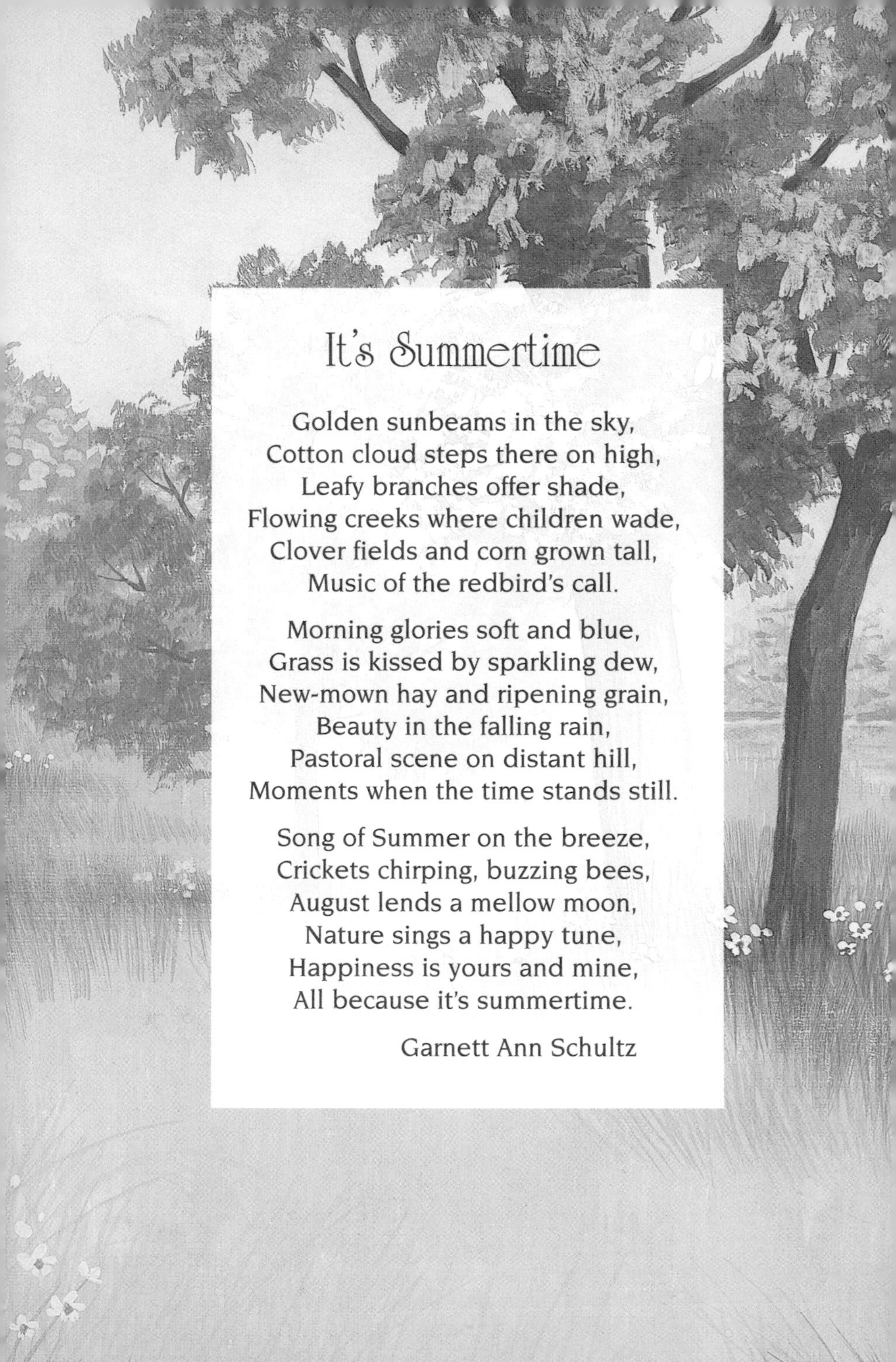

It's Summertime

Golden sunbeams in the sky,
Cotton cloud steps there on high,
Leafy branches offer shade,
Flowing creeks where children wade,
Clover fields and corn grown tall,
Music of the redbird's call.

Morning glories soft and blue,
Grass is kissed by sparkling dew,
New-mown hay and ripening grain,
Beauty in the falling rain,
Pastoral scene on distant hill,
Moments when the time stands still.

Song of Summer on the breeze,
Crickets chirping, buzzing bees,
August lends a mellow moon,
Nature sings a happy tune,
Happiness is yours and mine,
All because it's summertime.

Garnett Ann Schultz

Give thanks to the Lord,
invoke His name; make known
among the nations His deeds.
Sing to Him; sing His praise,
proclaim all His wondrous deeds.
1 Chronicles 16:8-9

Fall Ballet

The Autumn leaves are dancing
In gowns of gold and brown,
Silently, I watch from a window
As they swirl on sun-dappled ground.

The tempo of the ballet heightens
As the cold winds start to blow,
I watch the dancers vanish
In the flurry of falling snow.

But God has promised a springtime
With tiny, newborn leaves,
Again, I'll watch from my window
As they sway to a lullaby breeze.

But the beauty of Autumn will linger
Through Winter's dark days so cold,
And I will recall the glory –
The ballet of the brown and gold.

Sally R. Gottschling

Never Alone

You are never alone,
For God is always near,
In the quiet of your hours,
You should never have a fear.

For His presence is everywhere,
No matter where you are,
His light is always shining
Like the biggest, brightest star.

You are never alone,
When in your heart you know,
He is your true Companion,
Who cares and loves you so.

Jo March

Trust in the Lord forever!
For the Lord is an eternal rock.
Isaiah 26:4

Free for All

I saw you through the window,
Children of the tree,
Falling, falling, falling,
Ah, it was clear to me

That Autumn was upon us,
As Nature paid a call,
And Summer opened up the door,
Allowing leaves to fall.

Leaves like rain were falling,
Many at a time,
Golden, Autumn blessings,
Addressing, "Now, it's time."

Make ready for the harvest
Of "leavings" on the grass,
For many more will follow,
As Winter comes to pass.

There is ne'er a pausing
In Nature's free-for-all,
As Winter bows to Summer,
And Summer nods to Fall.

For always there are seasons,
Each one in harmony,
Giving, blending, lending,
Sweet gifts, and all for free.

Dolores Dahl

Wisdom

Wisdom comes from living,
From triumph and defeat,
Both smiles and tears are needed,
To make our lives complete.
We cannot teach another,
What we ourselves have learned,
Man does not comprehend until
He gets his fingers burned.
"For everything a reason"
Is hard to understand,
We have to follow God in faith,
And do the best we can.
We must not grieve for anything
We might have been denied,
No heart can have the room for God,
And still have room for pride.
So what if others treat us,
With malice and contempt,
Each of us must bear our cross,
And no one is exempt.
And yet with our acceptance,
Of everything God sends,
He promises us Heaven,
Where every sorrow ends.

Grace E. Easley

It's a Cause for Celebration

It's a cause for celebration
When Autumn walks the land,
Sprinkling miracles everywhere
Too grand to understand.

Nature wears a velvet gown
Of crimson trimmed with lace.
She waves a magic, golden wand
With elegance and grace.

Hearts fill to overflowing
As leaves begin to fall.
Too soon it will be snowing
As Winter comes to call.

Every pumpkin knows the secret,
But none will ever tell
How Nature works her magic
And holds us in her spell.

It's a cause for celebration
That brings me to my knees
As I catch a glimpse of God
Reflected in the trees.

Clay Harrison

Come, Let Us Share...

Lord of the harvest
And all that is good,
We thank You for
Thy gifts of food.

With warming sun
And gentle rain,
You've richly blessed
Our land again.

Our shelves and bins
And barns o'erflow
With harvest gifts
Thy hand bestows.

Still, there are those,
Now as we speak,
Who have little or
No food to eat.

And we should not withhold
But give,
To feed the hungry,
Where'er they live.

That all God's children
Will be fed,
Come, let us share
Our daily bread.

Kay Hoffman

*The Lord will give you the
bread you need and the water
for which you thirst.*
Isaiah 30:20

Winter Delight

The snow falls upon the pines,
And glistens like the stars,
Dainty snowflakes, gifts from Heaven,
Make my thoughts to pause.

No two of them are quite alike,
I've heard that through the years,
But, holding them briefly in hand,
Brings me close to tears.

Exquisite beauty that they are,
In an instant, they are gone,
What a joy! My hands can hold
A miracle of God.

Mary Ann Jameson

God's Creatures

God's creatures so small,
Some timid and white,
Some multi in color,
Some furry and bright.

The lamb in the pasture,
So precious and warm,
The deer of the forest
That love the acorn.

The cat by the fireside,
Curled up fast asleep,
Contented and loving,
And perfectly sweet.

The birds in the treetop,
Melodious sound,
Are God's chosen creatures,
He's chosen abound.

He cares for the lame ones,
The large and the small,
Provides for them shelter,
And loves one and all.

Katherine Smith Matheney

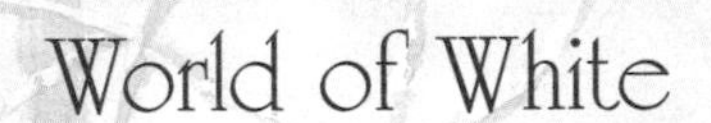

World of White

The morning was a true delight,
Everything on earth was covered white,
When I was a child, this would be
True magic and a thrill to me.

It was early morn with naught disturbed,
But small mammal tracks upon the snow,
Another world was taking place
As small feet would come and go.

They left their little tracks around,
And no one knew, for they made no sound,
Mounting snow made sculptures white,
And all of nature was alight.

One surely knew this different world
When snow on boughs blew softly down,
And every plant that held the earth
Wore a silver, shimmering crown.

Ah, yes… 'tis nature at its best
That I have seen before,
Just one of God's great miracles
And I'll always wish for more.

James Joseph Huesgen

I Walk With Him

By day and night, I walk with Him
Who guides my steps away from sin,
And every day, in every way,
He calms my heart against dismay;
He comforts me, on every lane
Where I must suffer grief or pain
And – when some hill is hard to climb –
He gives me strength, to join with mine.

I am, forever, in His care
To harvest joys we sow and share,
And blessed with love of Christian pride,
To have my Savior by my side;
It is a grace upon my life
To soothe each day of earthly strife
And grant my soul a Heaven's berth –
Because I walk with Him, on earth.

Michael Dubina

More Valuable Than Sparrows

If God's eye is on the sparrow
And knows should but one fall,
A bird so ordinary,
A bird so very small...

Then surely He sees each of us,
His watchful eye's on you,
For you are far more valuable
Than many birds, it's true.

God's precious and most priceless
Aren't the well-known in this life,
But those much like the sparrows,
The ordinary who know strife.

And in your strife, God's surely there
To mend and set you free,
Like a sparrow with a broken wing
That cannot leave its tree.

No need to worry or to fear
When God's made it crystal clear,
His eye is on the sparrow
And to us He's very near.

Gina Mazzullo Laurin

The Birds

Eagles, hawks and doves soar high,
Endlessly their home, the sky.
Perched on tree branch, housetop, too,
The wren and snowbird chirp their news.

Beneath the bush from glen to glen,
Hide the pheasant, lark and elusive hen.
Stop and listen as day begins,
Their happy chatter, your thoughts they'll win.

Geese and ducks on yearly flight
Join with swallows by day or night.
We do not ask or wonder why,
Their message given as they fly by.

God does not order or command
These pictures given throughout the land.
Go forth this day with happy thought,
God's heavenly creatures, their message brought.

Sophie Kleenman